May Contain Nuts

AF624543

Trevor Edge

BookLeaf Publishing

Presentation by *BookLeaf Publishing*

Web: www.bookleafpub.com

E-mail: info@bookleafpub.com

ISBN: 9789357445825

First edition 2023

To Dianna (aka The Missus), like a festival toilet, she seems cursed to be eternally engaged. Some would say I should make her an honest woman, to which I say, what's she been lying about now? But without her support, I would have fallen to the dark side long ago. Love you. X

ACKNOWLEDGEMENT

Thank you to all those who have inspired the words that follow. Many of you may have done this unintentionally and/or without knowingly giving consent. Although of course any similarities in the text to persons alive or dead is purely coincidental.

Also, to those who so kindly formed the genetic soup from which my life sprung, and those who have endeavoured to ensure that this life has continued and on occasion been entertaining.

PREFACE

Everyone's got a book in them. Which surprised me, because I didn't remember eating one. Perhaps it was all that was in when I returned from the pub. Could have been worse I guess? Well this one is mine. I hope you enjoy it, but please don't eat it. It may contain nuts.

Dedicated To

The one's who were there
When I threw out my toys and tore out my hair
Listened to all my grumbles and gripes
Endured the bitterness, the rants and the snipes
Steadied the ramparts and papered the cracks
Pushing me forward, whilst having my back

Then, of course, there were those who sought to derail
Booed my successes and prayed I would fail
Spreading their muck and sowing their doubt
Lies slyly whispered or insults they'd shout
But your blows to my body and ego have healed
Your efforts didn't dampen, they strengthened my zeal

So whether you backed me or stood in my way
You made me the man who stands proudly this day
For those by my side may we all raise a drink
And to those in the shadows, thanks a lot...You still stink!

The Last Train

We're all aboard and on our way
Our tickets stamped and no delays
The lucky ones may find a station
To jump before our destination
With every day the coals are stoked
Our lives' excess in a billowing smoke
Our failure to discern our needs from our greed
Powers The Train at calamitous speed
We know where we're heading, the future's at stake
Some try to re-route or to heave on the brakes
But The Train has momentum and the world's weight in tow
Our efforts have grown, but no signs we have slowed
A tunnel's upon us, the light behind left
Cling on to your loved ones and take a deep breath
For the days of mankind may have sadly elapsed
We've arrived to a new world. PLEASE MIND THE GAP!

0% Spirit

I sat in the bar where Oliver Reed died
I guess he was busy drinking with brethren
For his spirit failed to pass on by
He was probably raising some Hell up in
Heaven
I tried to channel Oscar Wilde
Per chance to find some inspiration
But sadly he found little to tempt him
In the desperation of my invitation
I laid out an entire buffet for Elvis
An array of American style delights
Yet on his celestial throne he remained
Refusing my myriad calls to alight
Friedrich Nietzsche I had not invited
But still he popped up and offered some words
He felt my quest for spectral assistance
Was at best weak, at worst absurd
"The dead have done their part and now
Can rest their voices and their souls.
Don't seek to stir them from their slumber
When you feel challenged by your goals.
The answers are neither upstairs nor down
They're found within and not without.
Refill your quill, re-click your pen,
Recharge your brain, get your finger out!"

And with that he left me on my own
Then the page magically ceased to be blank
The crafting of it was mine alone
And for that only myself to thank

The Loner

He's the kind of guy you wouldn't like
To run into down an alley at night
Or a street in the morn'
A car park at dawn
An avenue at noon
Or an unhappy hour in a Witherspoon
One who doesn't care for moments of mirth
Just longs to be given a wide birth
Leave him to his own devices
Make an effort not to catch his eyes, his
Gaze could curdle any cream
His image you'll find under M for mean
His scowl could turn your fresh bread green
Whatever happened in his past
I certainly wouldn't suggest you ask
Unless you want an uncertain future
In plaster cast, possibly with sutures
Simply avoid him at all costs
Streets…hell, even counties cross
This guy isn't a project
Nice at heart just needs respect
No there's no sun behind the clouds
Hear his cues and hear them loud
Not a sniff in the air of bonhomie
He doesn't want your company

Nor should you don't want to be in his
My last word of advice is this
Unless you want to be an unwitting blood donor
DON'T, ON ANY ACCOUNT, MESS WITH
THE LONER

The Night Life

On any suitable night, until dawn, they emerge
From their squalid dens and to watering holes they do surge
To drain the oasis they try and enriched by its spring
Onward to the rutting grounds their forms they eagerly fling
Some have dapper plumage or exotic calls to mates woo
Whilst others provoke with an extravagant hip thrust of two
A few having imbibed too much of the waters of life
May find their moves somewhat impaired, even paralysed
After hours of frenzied flirtation, libido permitting
Pairs seek safer places their coupling for the committing
Whilst others less fortunate gorge on some dry carcass meat
Before crying wails into the night and to their nests retreat
They're quick to recover, their next attempt won't be too long

Their egos and livers in early years still holding strong
But the Party phase of their lives soon passes before these pups' eyes
And their powers diminish far faster than they realise
So "My dear creatures of night I say go forth and go fast.
For the Moon's shining bright, let lunacy reign while it lasts"

The Tale of Guffer Fatbelly

Guffer was in a gentle repose
When he heard the calls of alarm
He grabbed his shiny sword and trident
His favourite pair of battle arms
As he approached the battlefield
His eyes drew wide as greeted
With a scene of devastation
Of fallen allies defeated
Their foes stretched out before them
In a line seemingly without end
But Guffer knew he must strike at the heart
His honour to defend
With berserker rage he roared
As his feral temper unleashed
Leaping forth he buried his trident
Deep in the belly of the beast
With a barrage of slashes and gouges
His sword carved the skin into shreds
His trident, enveloped in carcass,
He cried as he raised overhead
The crowd gasped, looking upon him
His victory proudly displayed
King Richard cried 'Freddy stop playing with
your food!
Look at the mess that you've made!'

Unofficial account – Battle of the White Hart Carvery– 1435 (or just after half 2 on Sunday)

Noooooo!

They nearly always come at night
Into my world they creep
A stirring in the darkness
That wakes me from my sleep
My mind so nearly settled
My comfort finally found
Yet somewhere from the silence comes
The slightest bothersome sound
My ears prick up, my brows furrow
A clenching of my teeth
The realisation they are back
I cry out in my grief
NOOOOOOOO!
This invasion of my mind
Forever from my slumber woken
No therapy will fix for me
My thoughts for they are truly broken
What cursed foes are these you ask
That strike without remorse?
My affliction? My burden? My scourge?
Ideas for poems, of course!

In Lincoln - Chapter 1

Dear Editor
First time writer, long time reader
Don't often complain, don't feel the need to
But hoping you might have the chance to advise
On a query I have re chocolate bar size
I don't often buy them, I'm certainly no addict
But it seems that they're neither as long or as thick
As previously produced, no brands will I name
It's across the board, they all seem to share blame
I know that my sight isn't as strong as it once was
But I'm certain they've shrunk, I can see it, because
I have a drawer for them, to the right of my telly
And it takes more bars to fill this…and my belly
They're taking the public for a ride is my thinking
Hope you can advise, Confused In Lincoln

Dear Editor
No response yet to my letter, guessing you're busy
Well regardless this time my query's more fizzy

The topic being new-fangled energy drinks
And how I've noticed some unsettling links
To post-imbibing bodily reactions
And thought you might feel that it warranted action
I'd normally choose a traditional type
I don't follow trends or listen to hype
But lately it seems I can only obtain
Some brightly labelled can with an obtuse name
And within an hour of drinking said liquids
With pulse rate increasing and flickering eyelids
I'm somehow quite frenzied and agitated
And I have to breath slowly till it has abated
I can only assume if repeated elsewhere
That some sort of chaotic event will occur
The world could erupt in the space of eyes blinking
But what can we do? Panicky in Lincoln

Dear Editor
Thankfully I still enter converse despite
Once more seemingly lacking any reply
As now it has come to my avid attention
Some changes in typical social convention
In particular, regarding the usage of phones
I recall that these once where confined to one's home
But now that they're mobile it raises the question

Of safety when using in transit...pedestrian
The younger amongst us seem constantly smitten
With playing, displaying or capturing their vision
I'm hoping this digital age is a phase
How sad their lives seem that they fail to engage
With the wonders around them, with all nature's beauty
I've tried counselling some, but their answers were snooty
It seems the sage wisdom I sought to impart
Merely warranted 'Clear off, you doddery old fart!'
Perhaps if they hear it from you it will sink in
Yours pessimistically, Ignored(?) in Lincoln

Dear Sir In Lincoln, just writing to say
Could you kindly stop sending such letters our way
We're a newsagents you see and I'm not an editor
Yes we deliver news, but writing…no credit there
Whilst we stock both the drinks and the chocolate you mention
We were not involved in their formula's invention
And as for the phones, yes, it's a sad reflection

On the world's beauties and how our juveniles neglect them
But please send your thoughts to a more relevant receiver
Yours awkwardly, Sunnydale Shop, Ms Weaver

Love In a Virtual World

It was an adventure that I didn't expect
Our pixels met across a crowded tavern
Like finding a Potion of Limitless luck
It was just too improbable to happen
Her beautifully rendered form
And totally unfeasible chest
Enveloped in tight tanned leather
And a gleaming armoured vest
A level 20 elven rogue
Could this ever really be?
A dwarf mage, barely level 4
Would she even notice me?
But to my surprise, my cheesy lines
Like an arrow, found their mark
I didn't cast a lightning spell
But there clearly was a spark
In days to come, we rode together
Through mountains and dark woods
We raided many a village
And she sometimes shared the loot
We battled our way through countless quests
And tore nations apart
But my only true desire
Was to conquer her wild heart
And then one day in the Lenstrine Hills

I dropped down to one knee
To ask her if this virtual love
Meant the same to her as me
"Of course!" she cried and stooped at once
To kiss my dwarven brow
"This is it" I thought, it's only right
I show my true form now
Flicked on my live cam'
Sadly in real life, I'm not that pretty
She did the same and to my surprise
There sat a butch male brickie

Chicken In a Fox Run

I was a chicken in a fox den
I snuck in through the back
And blended in as best I could
Hoping not to be attacked
My disguise was simply to act somewhat wild
With a stalking manner I hoped they would find
Convincing enough to survive for a while
If not kosher fox then somewhat vulpine
My plan was called Operation LifeSaver
For my coop had suffered many a loss
Stay under the radar, currying favour
Waiting to get my point across
Ingratiated in the skulk
Suggesting diet variants
Poultry's quite paltry, it's no good for bulk
Why not go veggie or pescetarian?
(Sorry to throw the fish in the mix
But 'Cluck out for yourself'
As we say in the chicks)

Despite raising snouts from some folks in the crew
I nearly gave a cry triumphant
When I thought my actions were bearing fruit
Well veg'… as the leader returned from the hunt

A glimmer of orange draping from her jaw
Could it really be, had she found us a carrot
But no, she went on to regale of the tale
How she'd raided a cage and picked up a parrot

My mission a bust and my co-habitees
Suspicious I might not be part of their troop
As they lay to sleep off their exotic feast
I ascended to light and flew home to my coop
The chicks were amazed, had assumed me deceased
And despite my failure they could understand
My dreams of somehow bringing peace
Were simply beyond this chicken's wingspan
We resigned ourselves to be vigilant
And at least for the moment we agreed
That despite my mission being a failure
I'm a chicken through and through, simply born to suck seed

Is It Friday Yet?

Is it Friday yet?
Till six hours in there is naught but a blur
Tearing at hair and you've no time to spare
Add to the pile the fresh jobs rushing in
Like fire alarms come the telephone's ring
Inquisitive bosses lurk ever closer
Keen to inject with a long prying nose
No, it's Monday

Is it Friday yet?
The caffeine can't fix this body clock
Which is running on empty and so deep in shock
The cogs, though they turn, find no rhythm still
There's a petulant mood, but the urge to kill
Has subsided a little, after Monday night's sleep
Though it's still somewhat hard your frail temper
to keep
No, it's Tuesday

Is it Friday yet?
So here we are at the peak of the week
With pace picking up, though the inclines still
steep
But you're still in first gear and there'll be no
free-wheeling

You find a mistake and your pulse hits the ceiling
And your heart skips a beat every time a job lands
In your supposedly capable, trembling hands
No, its Wednesday

Is it Friday yet?
Snoring in meetings, which serve to dictate
That you'll work till you're eighty, from half five till late
For a pension you thought would last you for years
But offers no change from a round of cheap beers
And your ex will take half for their days sat alone
While you furrowed your brow and worked fingers to bone
No its Thursday

Is it Friday yet?
End of the week, but you've still got till five
Your face offers no proof that you're still alive
Autopilot has taken control
You're daydreaming that you're back on the dole
You sprint for the door with two minutes to go
But you're stuck for an hour in the rush hour slow

But.....IT'S FRIDAY!

Shower and shaving, spray and then dress
Sweep back your hair, cause you need to impress
Swift shot or two while the taxi arrives
Ferrying you off to a cheap drinking dive
Swapping some words with a slapper from Kent
Ending up somewhere that you never meant
You'll pretend you're someone else if she ever calls
'Cause you've seen more attractive lavatory walls
Ringing your parents lest they ring you first
A Sunday morn' wake up call would be much worse
Watching the football and screaming till hoarse
Calling the ref something apt, but quite coarse
The night comes again and once more to the tiles
Vodka and mixer to flavour the bile
That you'll see once again in the hours before dawn
Between vows of eternal sobrierty sworn
Sunday lunch roast and an afternoon kip
48 hours in a memory blip
The alarm you hear now brings the suggestion
You should get a life, but once more comes the question
Is it Friday yet?

My Mother

She's got antique clocks and dirty socks
Behind the sink in a cardboard box
She's got shirts with collars that reach the cuffs
And skirts that once dropped barely enough
In a shed out back there's a draft of some play
With a name that sounds Scottish, but I dare not
say
There's some mouldy bottles of Hai Karate
And some nude pictures, not erotic, just arty
There's Hitler's diaries down in the cellar
Sandwiched between some old copies of Bella
There's some photos where she's kissing Elvis
A pair of fake breasts and a prosthetic pelvis
There's some body armour up in the attic
A joke shark fin and a snorkel...aquatic
There's my sweet cat Bob, disappeared '92
Fell in and preserved in my father's home brew
If Pandora's box held the evils of Hell
You can bet that she's kept, the guarantee as well
And there will be chaos like never before seen
On the day that my Mother decides to spring
clean

Maybe, One Day

Passed a tramp out on the street
Wearing bin bags on his feet
Looking strange, he begged for change
Can't catch the eyes of passers by
It starts to rain, he starts to cry
And he thinks maybe, one day
Things will pick up

Drove by a woman, barely dressed
Selling the figure with which she was blessed
Her early years are filled with fears and tears
Her torn clothes and broken nose
From where her pimp rained down the blows
And she hopes maybe, one day
She can just pack up and go

Saw a child disguised as a man
No parents to hold his thieving hands
No strict regime, no hopes, no dreams
Pumped full of drugs to stop the screams
And as the judge sends him down he wonders
Maybe, one day
Someone will understand

Saw a patient racked with pain
Counting the days that remain
Would trade all his wealth
For renewed health or a second chance
To sing and dance
And he prays that maybe, one day
He will pass gently away

Looked in the mirror at a fool
Who went to well-respected schools
Taught by the best, he passed the tests
But he grumbles now just like the rest
About the age of his car
And his grumbling ma
And his mumbling pa
And repairs on his home
And his out-of-date phone
And the TV repeats
And whenever his football team gets beat
And his wife and the strife
When he's woke by the baby and maybe, one day
He'll realise just how lucky he is

The Wildcard

I act like I'm quite horny
For any girl I'll try
My lines are old and corny
My wit more stale than dry
But the guys call me The Wildcard
The Joker in the Pack
Frustrated, even demented
By the love life that I lack

I joke to hide the sadness
I laugh to cloak the fears
My eyes show glints of madness
'Neath a film of held-back tears
Yet they all call me The Wildcard
The Joker in the Pack
Alone here in the darkness
Like the last spud in the sack

My knees aren't what they used to be
My vision's slightly blurred
I think old-school makes me look cool
My clothes sense is absurd
Still they all call me The Wildcard
The Joker in the Pack
Old, unused and broken down
Like a rusty country shack

I'm tired of the sideshow
The efforts to amuse
I wonder who I'm fooling
With this sad unending ruse
But I never liked The Wildcard
Or the Joker in the Pack
So like a broken boomerang
I've gone and I won't be back

Error Message

The techno generation, plug in for their salvation
To find a meaning to their cyber-souls
A misled generation, spoon-fed their information
By cuboid teachers with remote controls

This ill-taught generation, can't work out multiplication
The answers there for them in cell C4
A world web generation, with friends in every nation
But really they're a paedophile next door

Our mobile generation, can't hold true conversation
The words just don't flow right unless they're keyed
A PC generation, living in isolation
Their router's just a drip to feed their need

The console generation, can't play without a station
The days will pass them by without a thought
A slow degeneration to human vegetation
But should we confirm, retry or abort?

Just Good Friends

Just good friends, nothing more
No hint of flirting or amour
No knowing smile or secret glance
Suggesting feelings of romance

Just good friends, who think alike
Talking long into the night
Sharing feelings felt for others
And failings of respective lovers

Just good friends, feeling shattered
Sofa looking somewhat tattered
Pay no thought to sleep together
'Cause they both know they would never...

Just good friends, holding tight
A drafty flat on a winter's night
The heating isn't up too much
And they needn't fear each other's touch

Waking to a brand new day
For once they're lost for things to say
Never again to be the same
Two questions in their minds remain
Were they truly just good friends?
And was this just the beginning or an end?

The Odd Couple

I don't have fame and I don't have wealth
I don't have brains nor mental health
I don't have a six-pack, its more like a keg
I'm not real athletic, got short hairy legs
I can't make converse with upper class types
Or even eat my food without baby wipes
I can't keep time, 'cause I'm way too tardy
I'm easily lured by the smell of Bacardi
Don't have nice teeth, don't have soft hair
My laundry's stacked in a corner somewhere
I can't fix a leak in the bathroom ceiling
My pants are too tight and their holey revealing
She knows all this, yet she still endures
Doesn't look for a compromise or a cure
She likes me just the way I am
The best thing about me is I'm her man

Or so you'd think, but if you saw us together
You'd see she's quite common and none too
clever
She laughs at my lines, even ones that aren't
humerous
He past is quite shady, her skeletons numerous
She can't cook more than a plateful of beans
She always spends way beyond her true means

She stutters her consonants, slurs on her vowels
Wears vats of perfume, make up by the trowel
She walks like John Wayne after five hours riding
She takes several days simple answers deciding
In the ways of fashion clearly colour blind
Her jokes sometimes funny, but seldom kind
She picks her nose and she scratches her crotch
She looks like Babe Ruth, but she thinks she's Baywatch
But still...she brings me joy, she's a sweetheart, I love her
We both don't have much, but at least we've each other

School Report

We start with English, Mr Weasly
Looks like his name sounds, hair all greasy
Beady eyes and a thin moustache
Teeth worn down 'cause he tends to gnash
But putting aside his dubious appearance
He conveys his subject with great coherence
Even the most illiterate amongst us
Seem to have learnt a bit, so he gets a B plus

The geography teacher Mr Brown
Clearly comes from out of town
Or has some sort of speech impediment
'Cause every word is coated with phlegm
The kids sing loudly 'It's Mr Drowned
You need an umbrella when he's around'
Its hard to focus on tectonic plates
When you end up feeling like you've slept in a lake
'E's the best I can offer and that purely for
How the wash wakes me up, when I'm starting to snore

A 'D' for science, Mr Gough
Aka the Crazy Prof'
Keeps the lesson lively and fun

But can be reactive (pardon the pun)
Caught me once with Jenny Turner
Messing around with a Bunsen burner
Made us stay on after class
Emptying flasks of methane gas
Not a task I'd care to repeat
But other than that Mr G's fairly neat

Mr Grayson lectures on History
Like his marriage could well soon be
I heard from Barker in Class 3C
His missus ran off with Mrs McGee
Might explain the mood he's been in
He's been spotted crying alone in the gym
But education doesn't stop for sad tales
Like your love life, I'm afraid it's F for Fail

The man entrusted with Phys' Education
Also called Torturous Degradation
Is the sadist known as Mr Pratt
He doesn't care whether you're fit or fat
He'll run you until you hit the ground
His thirst for punishment knows no bounds
Frankly Sir, you're sick and strange
Your grade is 'D' as in 'deranged'

Maths is the realm of Mrs Fleck
Cursed with the most uninspiring subject
All sorts of things no-one will ever use

The topic all endure, but no-one would choose
Prime numbers? Fibonacci? Geometry?
No thanks for these lessons, but for effort a C

Onto French with Madame Dubois
The lady who's captured my hormonal heart
I've sat there beguiled for many a while
By her hazel eyes and her ruby lips smile
Her Ooh La La shakes me to my core
Oh Madame Dubois, it's you, je t'adore
On God's Green Earth there's simply no way
I could give her anything other than an 'A'

Another year over, your grades greatly range
With some high and mighty, some low you could change
But I can't tell you your job, I simply would rather
Sum up in these three words…Must try harder!

The Interview

His pulse is high, twitchy eyes, feels he's letting
His misgivings get to him, he's not ready
Into a personal hell he is heading
Barely walking through the door, legs of jelly
The panel wait, faces straight, paper and pens
He sits and squirms under their microscope lens
He's researched, done the work, just depends
If they spring something new on him, how he defends
Their eyes stare, deep within, into his soul
Derisory looks turning his blood icy cold
His hands shaking, words breaking, giving up hope
But his inner voice tells him "Just go for broke
The stage is all yours, its your turn to dance
Your time to indulge, sing your praise, sell your brand
No-one does it like you can, don't just sit there, take a stand!"

"For me this job hasn't been easy, in what seems like an eternity
And yet remains a mystery, I've never climbed the corporate tree
Content to stand back, lackadaisically

Never the star in the cast…but now that's history
My CV's impressive, I know you've read it
Maybe you thought it was lies, just an edit
Showing the work where I've never had credit
I want the acclaim, there, I finally said it
There's nobody better than me at what I do
You know this in your heads, it's not breaking news
I'm size 50 brogues, there's no-one fits these shoes
No need for this test, just acceptance of truth
If you finally stop taking talent for granted
The one's at the cliff face won't be disenchanted
Your management so far has been too high-handed
A seat at the top table is now demanded
So start a new era, let us all rejoice
Or see what we built can be easily destroyed
It's time that the silent were given a voice
Bless my appointment, make the right choice!

There's No Correct Answer?!

This simply makes no sense to me
Like one plus one would equal three
Or coffee being the same as tea
It doesn't stack up…logically
Sure, if you'd phrased so as to suggest
A level ranging from worst through to best
A gradient perhaps, from more through to less
But you wanted an answer, a no or yes
You weren't asking me to convey a vague rating
To the question that you were so badly relating
The fact is I hate that you're now debating
That rightness does not need my reply equating
For the analyst within me ensures that I say
That for binary questions, a yea or a nay
There should by return be some form of display
Be it condemnation or preferably praise
Note, if you struggle to endure hesitance
There's no benefit in your intercedence
For I will not accept that there's no relevance
And the fault lies with you and your lack of
patience
Whether you welcome my output positively
Or choose to react with more negativity
The answer will be reckonable, just you see

Now then what was the question? Ah yes, to be or not to be?
Hmm….

Thank you

I don't think I'll ever be top of this game
I've got meagre aims, far below global fame
I'd rather a leasehold than a household name
A short period of significant recognition
That would be more on my level of ambition
Then back to the shadows, a successful mission
A pub quiz question or a blast from the past
'Hey remember that guy, who once made us laugh
So hard I blew snot and your brother passed gas?'
Yeah, that's around the mark I'm looking to make
Not shelves of awards or sales records to break
Just climbing a hillock and planting a stake
I'm not revolutionary, no blood and thunder
I don't mean to tear the poetic world asunder
Though I wouldn't mind more than one hit to my wonders
A little more brass in my pocket perhaps
Enough to explore somewhat more varied maps
And to maintain the flow on my local's beer taps
So, if you've been searching for the next big thing
That woman or man, who'd be queen or be king

Don't back this horse 'cause you're not going to
win
Have a giggle, a cry, some other emote
Recommend to a friend, if my words float your
boat
I'll even allow you an odd line to quote
But the odd gig or two, spouting lyrics to a
crowd
I reckon that's my limit, one encore allowed
And then out of retirement I'll refuse to be
cowed
I hope you've enjoyed this outpouring of brain
Whilst you helped me a lifetime's objective
attain
Goodbye me, my dear reader, well…maybe I'd
do it again

www.ingramcontent.com/pod-product-compliance
Lightning Source LLC
Chambersburg PA
CBHW051740130826
49812CB00033B/945
* 9 7 8 9 3 5 7 4 4 5 8 2 5 *